Laurie Eaves is a writer and long-distance runner from the village of Yapton.

He began performing raps about acrobatic animals in the late noughties in Norwich, where he headed up UEA Open Mic before playing guitar (badly) in Lyrical Ballads Cabaret.

In 2014, Laurie moved to London and learnt that not every poem has to be a mile-a-minute rhyming rant. He started speaking more slowly, performing regularly across the capital and beyond.

His work has been anthologised by Poetry Rivals, Bad Betty Press, Allographic Press, GUG Press and Spoken Word London, and featured in videos for Muddy Feet Poetry, Process Productions and Team UK Youth Cycling.

He works regularly with The Poetry Takeaway, writing poems for strangers across the UK from the back of a burger van.

Today, most of Laurie's poems are grit-and-honey pop songs about break-ups, tidying and weightlifting. He co-hosts the *Dead Darlings* podcast and co-produces the Vogon Poetry Slam.

He's been described as 'organised' by three people this year.

Biceps

Laurie Eaves

Burning Eye

This edition published by Burning Eye Books 2020

www.burningeye.co.uk

@burningeyebooks

Burning Eye Books
15 West Hill, Portishead, BS20 6LG

ISBN 978-1-911570-81-3

Biceps

For you

CONTENTS

I

MAKE

THE STORY'S BETTER
WHEN YOU TELL IT

Both versions start the same:
two twenty-somethings emerge

from Milan station into sweltering sunshine.
Stop to fill bottles for the walk to the hostel.

All gospel so far. Our descriptions of him are
usually similar: tall, olive skin, raggy T-shirt.

I normally add long nails, grit underneath.
You always mention sandals, loose Velcro.

He speaks Italian at me. I smile,
moving naïvely to shake his hand.

I don't remember if he punched me or whether I
just think he did because that's how you tell it.

I do remember the split second he tore the bumbag
from my jeans, snapping my belt. Thinking

    it's only money,
        then: passports.

I have absolutely no idea why I chased him.
Somehow in both versions I catch him.

In your story, I rugby-tackle him to the ground,
wrestle the bumbag from his grip and he runs scared.

In my head, he puts the whole thing down his pants.
He trips. My first memory of this city will always be

shoving my hand down the front of a stranger's
trousers and escaping with my life.

When you tell it, you say you worried I'd have an
asthma attack. I'm not sure I was breathing at all.

You call it the moment you knew I was your one.
I think of it as the day I lost trust in open spaces.

You finish by looking deep into my eyes.
I quip, 'So we got the Metro after that.'

You call me brave. I've never been
more terrified in my life.

The story's better when you tell it.
I've forgotten which version is true.

TINDER

We meet in the cinnamon
and cider of Bonfire Night.

Stick together, two toffee apples
in my detective overcoat,

sparks crackling between our cardigans
as the bottle rockets burst.

Smoke trails slip sideways
with the years.

Each anniversary, we snaffle ginger cake
from my pocket on Jamaica Road,

share 50p cups of tea
and terracotta skies.

When our friends find new flames
from the office or online,

you loop your burnt umber
hair above your ears,

squeeze the space
between my fingers.

Reminding me
of two teenagers

scribbling the start of a story
with sparklers,

etching their names
onto the night.

The only tinder burning
at the bottom of the bonfire.

IF THE SKY SHOULD FALL

I always say 'I love you.'
When you close the door
or fall asleep.

Don't need you to say it back.

But if the sky should fall
or if the rug gets pulled out
underfoot

I'd want you to know
more than anything in the world:
you're loved.

RECHARGING

Some nights we sit inside.
Sometimes I regret that.
Think of the memories
we could make:

hurting our cheekbones watching
stand-up in cellars, hearing poetry
that turns us inside-out, discussing
the finer points of brutalism
under gallery strip lights.

When this happens, I sip my tea.

Remind myself that just sitting
with you, learning how each
muscle in your body works,
is the biggest adventure.

APOLOGY FOR A DREAM

'You were so nasty to me in my dream just now.
    Turned blue saying the meanest things.'

'But it was a dream… I didn't really mean it.'

'Maybe you did mean it… subconsciously.'

'But it was your subconscious, not mine.'

'You don't get it.'

'Would it help if I said sorry?'

'…I think so.'

'Shuffle over a sec, then… I'm sorry I upset you in your dream.
    Forgive me?'

'…OK.'

'Better?'

'A bit.'

HIGHBURY & I

You crumple into our red rug.

Shoulders shrug, first slow bounces, then heaving shakes. Your body makes noises I've not heard before.

I give you my stale water. The ball of your throat bobs as you gulp. Hand me your phone, open on a memo. I read it twice. You've misspelled *sorry* – only one *r*.

Your lungs reset, louder when filling than pushing air out. I come to carpet level, hand you your cup: 'Your tea'll get cold.' 'It's water,' you swallow.

I choose to treat symptoms: say I'm upset you lied about staying at your mum's. Nothing more. Voice unraised, I ask if you still want to be with me. You nod.

I keep calm, complicit. Push my heart rate to a steady one-two. '*Only Connect* is on in a bit. Why don't you go change? I'll warm up dinner.'

We stand, silently separating.

SPLIT

A couple come
to a split in
the subway:
two tunnels
leading to
separate
roads.

They share
a single set of
earphones,
the wire
between
stretching
tighter
as they
approach.

At the split,
the thread
threatens
to slip
or snap.

But doesn't.

The couple
stop. Turn to
one another,
working out
where they're
going.

HULL

The Portsmouth of the North.
I sing 'Highway to Hull' all the way. You don't.

We're greeted by a street of 99, 98 and 97p shops.
I make a cut-throat sign on my neck. You look the other way.

We get lunch in The Real Sandwich Company. 'Sick of those
fake sandwich companies,' I wink. Your crust is soggy.

By the Humber, tobacco warehouses erode into the types
of pie shops where each pie has a Christian name.

As wind whips off the river, I tie the belt of my coat through
your elbow's crook: 'Don't want you to blow away.'

There's a Beautiful South poster at the ferry port:
Blue is the Colour. The salt in my lungs brings

back the sandcastle towns where I grew up,
always on the edge of being washed away.

I feel at home. Try to explain this to you,
but my words are whisked into the wind.

CROSSING

The piano player in the ferry bar
    has the best job in the world: murder
      'Layla', wake up in Amsterdam, get high,
    back on the boat. Between songs,
   you lay your fingertips on my knuckles:
  'I think I'd like to see her again.'
The boat rocks a little, then settles.
   A buoy flashes green somewhere in the sea.
     It makes me think of a traffic light.
            Go.
       'OK,' I manage.
  'OK as in *that's OK*, or OK as in *I understand*?'
 'Both. I think.'
We listen to the waves as the piano
  player moves from 'Lola' on to 'Delilah'.
   I bench-press the edges of my lips up:
    'It would probably help to tell me her name.'
     My mind sprints through names. They all end
      in *la*. I blame the piano player. You share her
   name, the click in the middle catching
  in your throat. It feels small.
  The piano player is taking requests.
'We should ask if he knows "The Piano Player Has No Talent".'
   'Mean,' you say. As we walk to our windowless cabin,
     a knot of mariner's rope rolls around
    inside my belly, unmoored.
   Convince myself it's seasickness.

ORANGE

'To divide is not to take away.'

PB Shelley

Say we grow oranges in the garden.
Always share them, half and half.

Suppose you give one of
your segments to a friend.

Watch their lips shrink as they roll
the juice around their tongue.

You come home fresher,
ready to get back in the garden.

I still have all my segments;
they still taste just as sweet.

CHICKEN RUN

The only time it upsets me
is when you're late for
the matinée of *Chicken Run*.

Midday Coke bubbles
burst in my belly
as I tell stale mates

you stayed the night
at a friend's
(technically true).

Your heels click in time
as Ginger throws her sprout
at the coal-scuttle wall.

Forty minutes in, I'm
Mr Tweedy and the
chickens are revolting.

'Finally something we agree on.'
Your Lancashire lilt stays
stubbornly Southern.

When the old crate flies
the fence, I wonder what lies
the other side of a Plasticine sunset.

ALRIGHT?

The last few months
Call and response
'Alright?'
'Not bad thanks, you?'
'Just said yes.'
You dump your peanut
of a fold-up chair.
the chair over later on,
As you take out
I rinse yesterday's tea
the one you spotted
and I snuck
Brought your tea
that evening,
I try to remember
you grinned
Microwave chilli
On cue,
I say it's hot
but not hot
Mouths full, we circle
Start the next round:
'Yeah, alright. You?'
I never listen
try to tell you
You never listen
but we both feel
the flat up
Pudding is
You look quizzical
like a fly's landed
I offer to nip

it's become our chorus.
at 6pm sharp.
'Alright?'
'Yeah, alright thanks. You?'
'Oh, right. Sorry.'
butter coat on the back
Sometimes this tips
making us jump.
your elephant earrings,
from your Moomin mug,
in Loose's cookshop
back to buy.
over in it
totally straight-faced.
the last time
like that.
or spag bog.
you ask if it's hot.
as in hot hot
as in spicy hot.
each other, boxers in a ring.
'So… alright?'
'Yeah, alright. Up to much?'
to what you say next,
about my day instead.
to what I say,
better for warming
with noise.
always yoghurts.
when I tell you,
on your lips.
to the Co-op,

trainers half-on.
my mouth moves
I stop short,
on my tongue.
'OK, babe,'
There might be
between here
'I love you!'
You say something, muffled

At the front door
mechanically: 'I…'
love you
'…I'll just be a mo.'
you reply offstage.
a massacre
and the corner shop.
I shout.
by the living-room door.

HOW DO YOU KNOW?

Because I like exploring with you: hiking through new cities
    or just making a mess in the kitchen.

Because you rub my legs when I've worn them out roller-skating,
    hoover the bit under the bed that makes me sneeze.

Because you find cookbooks for me in Oxfam,
    pick up trousers that actually fit me.

Because your skin is soft. I like skimming the smooth patch
    on your arm where you burnt yourself boiling eggs as a child.

Because your name feels natural in my mouth,
    like it's always been there waiting to be spoken.

'Just do, I suppose. You?'
    'Yeah… same, I guess.'

This is the part where we should pull our pillows together.
    'Shall I get the light?'

MARX & ENGELS

We're in a diner called Marx & Engels.
Despite its namesakes, there's a bill to pay.

Your right hand enters your PIN, as your left
slides me a card starring a sausage dog in a hat.

Inside, the card reads *Birthday Sausage.* This is the second
sausage dog birthday card you've given me.

You like sausage dogs. We have a pretend one at home
called Linda after Linda McCartney sausages.

There's also a two-pack of socks: one with foxes, one plain.
I think of the presents we used to give each other:

the bobble hat you bought at Gatwick Airport when I
said my ears were cold, the time you wanted ice cream

but I didn't know what flavour you liked yet so turned
up on your doorstep with five different litre tubs.

I don't remember when our presents became gifts:
bath bombs for birthdays, calendars for Christmas.

Back at our rented mattress, you wear your
reindeer bottoms with the hole in the crotch.

'You have a hole in your crotch.'
'I know.'

'Are you in a sexy mood?'
'I could be.'

Up close, your hair smells like London.
The red barbs beneath your belly button

catch my fingertips: stroking a cat
the wrong way, tail to tip.

I think of one night on my parents' sofa,
the goldfish watching us with glazed disgust.

This is the bit when you usually sit up.
But tonight you lie still, arms pointing

a path to your phone.
You have a message.

We stop: shy, shivering strangers.

INTIMATE HEALTH

How is your intimate health?
Do you have an itch down there?
No, not that far down,
stop at your gut.

Does it still get the ferris wheel flutter?
Or is it more solid? A knot of rope
you've lost the end of.

Have you gained weight since they moved in?
Grown a layer of love, pressing down
like oil on water?

How is your intimate health?
Is there a problem down there?
No, not that far down,
stop at your heart.

Does it beat alongside theirs
or has it fallen out of time?
Two metronomes side by side
drift out of sync naturally.

When you first lay together
did you stay up listening
to their breathing?

Does your own heartbeat echo
off your pillow nowadays,
drowning them out?

How is your intimate health?
How are you doing down there?
No, not that far down,
stop at your mouth.

Does it say *I love you* to smother the silence?
Do you still laugh at the same moments?
Can you describe their taste?

How is your intimate health?
Do you need help down there?
No, not that far down,
stop at your eyes.

Do your irises still sparkle
when they come home at 4am
with sick in their hair?
Not give the game away?

Are all your photos carbon copies?
Are you getting square eyes?
Can you see a future?
Are they in it?

ROOIBOS

Six years in
I'll offer you
rooibos tea
and you'll say,
'Don't you know me at all?'
and I'll drink
the whole pot
down to dregs
and sad lemon
looking for
the answer.

CHECK

The first time, it's an accident. You leave your phone in the bathroom and I catch it flashing *what's the deal with you two?* I never knew we had a deal. But after seven years studying, I know exactly how your thumb glides across the glass. When you knock I shout, 'I'm on the loo.' Pretend to watch the grouting. Decide to let you back in.

The second time, it's a mistake. As you shower, your alarm wakes me and I can't work out how to turn it off without opening your messages. I'm still struggling when I hear the water drain.

By the third time, I can remember the order your apps are open. How to stack them back together, happy families.

About now I come clean. Promise to stop.

Your email's easy enough, though your password isn't the park where we met any more. Within a week, your cookies crumble and you're finally an open page. Years shed like shoulder-skin as I scroll back to the start. Swallow piping rooibos tea, start a story by someone I've not met before.

I don't want to fix this. I want to be right.

EMBER

In spring, I push my pudding bowl
into a David Lynch quiff and it sticks.

Find I know how clothes work,
so they fit and feel good.

Discover how to lose and regain
jobs without missing rent.

You cut your lion mane
into a summer bob.

Call yourself a feminist
for the first time.

Learn to spot when you're upset
with me and when you're just upset.

In the shade of a swollen autumn oak,
we shed our teenage tongues.

Become partners.
Get a joint account.

Then one winter, we sit either
side of an underfed bonfire.

Stare into each other's eyes
as the final flames flicker.

Both searching for the
youth we once adored.

DEADHEADING

I feel you untangling
your roots from mine,

leaving tracks in the soil.
Spreading out to fresh ground,

finding new spots for
shoots to spring up.

In bloom, our colours
were so bright.

I can't help thinking:
if we'd snipped it sooner

something beautiful
might have grown.

Not just these deadheads
waiting for the scissors' cut.

II

BREAK

WAKE

Turn your head to the left,
see her sleeping. Rise together.
She boils the kettle, a sliver

of milk in her Moomin mug.
Suggests a chat. Take your
usual spots on the sofa.

She tears the world in two.
Silence, then sounds you've
never made before: animal.

The front door closes, the whole
house ages. Stare at cold tea,
anniversary cards still up:

two hedgehogs hedgehugging.
Come up for air. Walk somewhere,
anywhere. Get a chain coffee

in a part of town you hate.
Try to say *coconut flat white*
through pencil-thin lips.

Back home, watch the walls
'til she comes 'to get things'.
More tea, usual spots.

Watch *Bake Off*, joke about
Selasi's flat bottom. Think of
the birthday cake she made you

in the shape of a record player.
On the front step, she stands
sepia-tinted, suitcase in hand.

'I love you.'   'You too.'
Both know that's not enough.
Inside, the ghost

of a hairdryer sets you off.
Call your mum, hear her dreams
shatter into static. Back to bed.

Wish you could wake,
turn your head to the left,
see her sleeping.

PHANTOM

Two nights later I dream you
climb in next to me, pull my
body in to yours. As I sleep,

the part of my brain that
processes touch works over
time: feels your fingertips

brush each blackhead
on my back, my shoulders
tilt as you slip me across

the sheets, your chin
nestling in the crook
of my collarbone.

They say when you lose
a limb you still feel
its weight.

THE LIFE-CHANGING MAGIC OF TIDYING

When you come to collect your things,
you ask if I've read *The Life-Changing Magic of Tidying*.
I haven't.

You say the secret is laying out
all the objects in your home,
weighing each one in hand.

If they spark joy, you keep them.
If not, you have to let them go.

I wonder if one night as I slept
you pressed your palm to my back
and made your decision.

SISYPHUS' SUITCASE

He packs up all his troubles:

the fox socks with the hole in the toe,
the bumbag with the bust zip, the Beautiful
South poster that kept falling down.

All in the purple suitcase with the wonky
wheel, ready for a new life somewhere else.
Outside, he drags the suitcase behind.

It catches on the kerb, slips from his grip.
He doubles back. Stands in the pit
of the pavement, pushes instead.

The suitcase still gets stuck on the slope,
tumbles down. No matter how hard he pushes
or pulls, his old life rolls back to his feet.

FINAL FANTASY

In Norwich Oxfam there's a copy of *Final Fantasy XIII*.
Far from the best one.

On the case, there's a note in black permanent marker:
For my girl and my world, love Jamie xxx

It's going for £8.

MOVING

The girl in the fuchsia Converse stands in our front room,
twiddling the broken cord of the sash windows. It snapped
months or years ago. She asks if anything comes with the flat.

I wonder why she'd want shelves full of frames but no photos.
Three Kid Creole and the Coconuts albums, framed lopsidedly,
too scratched to play.

Stripy bedroom curtains that never quite matched the bedsheets
with the blue beach huts. I say she can have the dining table.
I found it in a skip.

Fuchsia Converse leaves to meet her boyfriend.
He works in HR systems management.
I don't know what that is.

She never asks why I'm moving. Perhaps she's too polite.
I go back to my front room, knowing this will always be
the room, the building, the road.

I hope Fuchsia Converse moves in with her HR systems manager.
That they make this their front room. And when they leave
it's because they're ready to move on together.

KITCHEN SINK

When we moved in, my mum
said the pipe under the sink dripped.
Put a bowl under, told us to ring

the landlord Monday. Instead we
buried the pipe behind the carrier bag
where we kept the other carrier bags.

Still it dripped away.
Day after day.

When I leave, I dump the carrier bag
where we kept the other carrier bags
in a big bin bag out front.

Find the bowl brimming over,
sinking through a hole in the
chipboard: a perfect circle

of sodden sawdust collapsing
under its weight. We never
noticed 'til it was too late.

BEACHBALL

miss you like a beachball

flail useless limbs trying to catch you

jump to get closer

find my mouth full of sand

as you fly past into someone else's arms

III

BUILD

JOEY

You start out no more
than a kidney bean.

Crawl your way up to
the comfort of a pouch.

Soon you sprout roots
that become firm-muscled

legs, a long nose, triangle ears.
Eventually you have a head.

Grow tall enough to peek out.
Half-in, half-out, you take your

first long look. Choke on fresh air.
There is so much world, just outside.

Shrinking, you bury back into the
safe warmth. There will be days

when you'll wish more than anything
to return here: to be nothing.

So take your time. The world will still
be here when you're ready to jump in.

PUFFERFISH

Stress is a pufferfish. Starts out small,
    then swells bigger and bigger in my head.

Sometimes it grows so enormous
    I can see the spines.

But no matter how big it balloons
    it never ever pops.

I try to remember: although things seem huge
    and scary now they won't always be that way.

I just need to let some pressure out. Squeeze the fish
    tightly 'til it wilts back to its normal size.

One day I'll look back at it. Laugh at how cute
    it seems now and smile as it swims away.

RUNNING

starts when I
    fail to meditate.
        Try to clean
            my mind with
                a bucket and sponge
                    when it's a water
                        cannon firing back.

At night,
    the echo of my
        heartbeat on
            my pillow keeps
                my eyes wide.

My brain is an
    oozing wound
        praying for soothing
            sutures.

                A cure.

Dan at work runs.
        I have legs.
        I can do that.

At home,
    I pull on my jeans;
        I have no shorts.
            Tie up my
                flat-soled trainers,
                    head out the house.

I don't know
    how a kilometre
        works yet, just
            move quicker
                than normal.

My brain
    is so busy
        avoiding an asthma
            attack, it can't
                process anything else.

                After thirty minutes
            I stop, halfway round a park.
                Calmer.

Months race by
    underfoot,
        pounding my panic
            into the pavement
                each time I need
                    to hit pause.

Learning to stay upright,
        putting one foot
            in front of the other.

BICEPS

On a whim,
I buy a thirty-kilo
set of weights in Argos.
The polo-necked shopkeeper
asks how I'll get them home. I wave
at my wonky purple suitcase. He snorts.
I haul the weights back to the flat, count this
as my first workout. Take my puffer
twice. Find a video online of a
buff American instructor. He
calls himself Coach and
probably eats whey
protein.

For the next
twelve weeks, I learn
to tell dumbbells from
barbells, biceps from triceps.
Feel my upper back muscles for
the first time in twenty-seven years.
Wear shorts in winter, even when the
boiler breaks. Become better. Start
feeling a discipline I've been
missing my whole life:
a pen is a lot lighter
than your own
bodyweight.

THE CURE

There's a simple cure-all for everything,
a single, one-size-fits-all solution:

take	all the energy you waste hurting yourself and
turn	it to healing yourself
drink	apple juice instead of cider
flush	your smoky lungs with mountain air
get	high on exercise, punk rock and poetry
don't sleep	with people you don't respect
	if the world isn't showing you love
show	it so much love it's embarrassed
	into reciprocating
make	more time for your friends, always
buy	birthday presents
go	to gigs on your own
don't wait	to be asked
know	yourself
write	so much your wrists ache
run	so fast your body begs for broccoli
bring	your brain and body together in natural tandem
remember	you were not built to be caged in an office
	or trapped watching boxsets in bedsits
	you're an animal
act	like one

TANDEM

On Upper Street, a woman pedals a bicycle made for two.
Damned if she's going to let it go to waste.

OPENER

I open a jar by myself.
First time in years.

No silently handing you
lime pickle or jam, pretending
you're stronger than me.

Your eyes don't shine
childlike at the pop.

I enjoy the tension and release.
Eat the salty sundried tomatoes
inside. They're delicious.

PICKLING

The couple next door to me pickle.
As a verb.

Sit in the kitchen for hours,
pickling together.

He slices beetroot, she
pours white vinegar.

Both say 'I love you'
in outdoor voices.

They have half an animal
clingfilmed in the freezer.

Thaw bits of it on the side.
I've seen a claw on the counter,

talons unclenching
over an afternoon.

They spend every evening inside,
preserving life for later.

Nostrils blocked to the sharp
stench as it ferments.

LIME

'To divide is not to take away.'

PB Shelley

I throw out the bedsheets
we chose together, the ones
with the blue beach huts.

In with the baked beans
and bin juice, too far
gone for recycling.

Stuff new pillows into
lime green cases, freshly
washed in non-bio.

Think of a poem
I studied at A-level.
Choose to twist its meaning.

To divide is not to take away.
I'm still here.
Whole.

SELFIE

You always take the photos.
Remind me to smile:
'No, do it properly.'

I try my hardest.
You say I still look sad.
That makes me sad.

You buy a framed photo
for Christmas, shot by
a stranger in Hull.

You look happy.
I probably look sad.
I put the picture up.

On New Year's Eve you
hide it, mumble something
about tidying.

By February our sitting room
is a shadow, guts ripped out,
save a single photo album:

a scrapbook of Polaroids,
pamphlets and Eurostar tickets,
captions biroed in the margins.

As our parents wait
in two overstuffed cars,
I ask if you want it.

You don't. I take it with me,
just in case. In June, I write
at my neat new desk, look

out over a lawn where
naïve green tomatoes take
their first tinge of red.

The album sits Sellotaped shut
at the bottom of my bookcase,
all the sad versions of me

gathering dust.

THREE TEXTS FROM YOUR DAD
(A FOUND POEM)

22:38   Hey babe. Hope you kept some of the profiteroles.
            Can't wait to get home and lick them off your body.

63

09:22   Sorry Laurie. That wasn't meant for you.

09:24   Obviously.

MUSCLE MEMORY

'How are you?'
First time you've
asked in months. I act
the entertainer. Keep it light,
share my schedule. List the bands
I've seen. Let the ones you like linger
on my tongue. You smile through the
static. Sound well. We reach our tubes
almost in sync. As our signal slips away,
we plan an abstract coffee, both agree
'that sounds nice'. On the escalator,
my mouth outruns my mind: 'OK,
love you, byeee!' My body
sinks, guts hitting the
floor first. You're a
muscle memory.

ABSTRACT COFFEE

Speaking with you again
is dropping a needle
on a record that's
always been
spinning.

IMAGINE

Emily tells me she remembers
    the two of us as John and Yoko.

I'm not sure if this means
    you taught me to breathe.

If we spent too long in bed
    from the minute we met.

If I cut you 'til there was
    nothing but a body left.

Or if she knows: some nights
    I sang you to sleep with 'Imagine'.

Still lullaby each vowel
    so it sounds like your name.

SILVERSMITH

In Loose's cookshop, I check out
the expensive crockery. There's a jug
with *custard* printed on it.

The shelf below has a mug saying *bastard*.
'Custard bastard. Just like you, Dad.'
Dad moves to clip my ear.

As I dodge, you step out
of the stairwell and
my guts catapult.

Ten years ago, I kissed you
so hard in The Arun View,
the barman kicked us out.

Caught my tongue between your two
front teeth. I'd never done it before,
had no manual for my lips.

You taught me the real joy of sleeping
with someone: being utterly vulnerable
in the dark afterwards.

When I asked what you wanted to be
when you grew up, you answered,
'Silversmith,' no hesitation.

Now, you step out amongst
the silicon egg timers
(for timing your silicon eggs).

Your coat might be the same one
you wore last time we met, but the
brooch on your breast looks new.

I wonder if you made it
as I dash into the lift.

DIVORCEE

In her French garden, my cousin Marie
shares beefsteak tomatoes and her heart:
a patchwork of restitched soul.

Each seam a lesson from life,
Kevlar hemmed in the folds.
Tougher, not hardened.

She stretches out on her plastic
patio chair. Savours every grain
of sea salt on her tomatoes.

Feels late evening sun warm
the blood in her fingers, at ease
with herself and the world.

Knows the answer to every
question is A, B or C. Settles
wars before they begin.

    (Anyone who knows what to do in a crisis
    has probably been through a few.)

No need to search the globe
or her mind to find herself.
She's right here.

A GOOD BOOK

On the last page,
I lay my palm flat.

Inch down line by line,
afraid each word will
bring the end.

When I hit the final
full stop my heart
grows a hole.

At first the sun
seems shallow,
but in time burns
brighter than before.

I'm glad you lent
your book to me,
let me lose myself
in your story
for a while.

It's shown me truths
I never knew.

Now it's time
to swap back.

To dig out the book you
once borrowed from me,
lovingly dog-eared from
years in your bag.

You looked after it well.

Thanks.

LINER NOTES

Firstly, thanks to my mum for her patience in drawing about three hundred tandem bikes for the cover. And to my dad, brother Jake and sister Josie.

An enormous thank you to Laurie Bolger for being the first person to say 'I want to read your book.' If this book were a record, she'd be the producer.

Thanks to my earliest editors Hannah Gordon, Hannah Chutzpah and Hattie Grünewald for all spotting the typo in 'Portsdown Hill' (which got cut anyway).

Thanks to Bridget, Clive, Shagufta, Josie, Kate, Lucy and Harriet at Burning Eye for filling the top shelf of my bookcase with so many life-melting books. I still can't believe this is one of them.

This book is dedicated to Emma Molineaux-Inglis and Debbie Stathinaki – the two teachers who taught me to love language – and to the People's Poet, Rik Mayall.

Many of these poems started from exercises in Tim Clare's *Couch to 80k Writing Boot Camp* (timclarepoet.co.uk). Others came out of exercises at Words Down – a writing workshop that meets every Tuesday at 19:30 in Rubio, Harlesden, London.

Thanks to everyone in the prestigious White Swan Writing Workshop, including Amy Fox, Hattie Grünewald and Jo Thompson (who are all mean and funny), and Callum Hughes, Bethan Williams, James Sykes and Catherine Goldstone (who are all not mean but not funny), and Nicole Etherington (whose meanness to funniness ratio is as yet undecided).

I'm very grateful to everyone in Maddie Godfrey's Tell Me About Your Month Facebook group for helping me cut the quality control and actually do some words.

Thanks to Bad Betty Press for publishing 'Rooibos' in their *Alter Egos* anthology, to Amy Acre for her advice on white space and to Roger Robinson for telling me it wasn't done (it wasn't).

Over the last ten years I've been lucky enough to read at a bunch of amazing poetry nights. I've loved every single one, but have to give special shout-outs to Forget What You Heard (About Spoken Word), Spoken Word London, Genesis Poetry Slam, Boomerang Club, Bang Said the Gun and Allographic.

Thanks to Ian MacKaye, Bob Mould and Henry Rollins for always being there, and to PB Shelley for posthumously letting me butcher his poem 'Epipsychidion'. These poems wouldn't have been as short without the songs of the Minutemen or as beautiful without the novels of Carson McCullers.

Thanks to Chris 'Godhammer' Ogden, Hasina Allen, Rebecca Cooney (for poetry-midwifing 'Imagine'), Simon Robson, Tom Nguyen and George Banks (for not freaking out when I woke him in a Tokyo hostel to tell him this was being published).

And finally, to Imogen for the stories…

www.ingramcontent.com/pod-product-compliance
Lightning Source LLC
Chambersburg PA
CBHW032123050726
47590CB00008B/2942